HUMAN RESOURCES

A Practical Guide on Effective Workplace Management

By

Sandra L. Jean, Esq.

About the Author

Establishing The Jean Consulting Group on the foundation of integrity, Sandra Jean is a renowned Labor & Employment Attorney, HR Executive, and Philanthropist with over 25+ years of experience driving new levels of discourse rectification, team unification, and overall organizational success. Specializing heavily on the intricacies of people, process, and leadership, Sandra brings with her an extensive history spearheading all aspects of human resources, compliance relations, and cultivating healthy workplace cultures via leading with a moral compass. In addition, Sandra enjoys leveraging that dynamicity to not just deliver her clients the concierge representation and support they deserve, but she does so all while propelling various community initiatives forward along the way.

Throughout her career, Sandra has built a large inventory of experiences that became the catalyst for her endorsed standing as a business executive and as a philanthropist in her community. Prior to forming The Jean Consulting Group in early 2022, Sandra began her career as a dual compliance specialist and labor attorney supporting Beverly Enterprises and Golden Living in the New England area. With this as her base, Sandra soon capitalized more on her passion for people by holding executive roles within the human resources and employee relations spaces. Using her accounting background as leverage, Sandra ascended to an Area VP of Operations and Labor/Employment Relations role overseeing a $96M annual budget and consulting with providers across four states. She later scaled to become a VP of HR and In-House Counsel overseeing all legal and operational matters relating to workforce management.

Performing this role at Community Health Services of Georgia, Sandra oversaw HR programs that supported 6,500+ employees in 62 nursing statewide. In 2020, Sandra accepted a Senior VP of HR role with Diversicare Healthcare Services, which is a national provider of long-term care services. Throughout her career, Sandra became renowned for devising and implementing human infrastructures that led to maintaining an exceptional workforce across the several states she supported, increasing overall hire rates by 33% and retention and engagement.

Now blending her competencies of people-centric processes, governance, community networking and firm belief that strong results stem from strong teams to form The Jean Consulting Group, Sandra has attained a reputation for influencing measurable results and sustainable business trajectories. Furthermore, securing brand images as advancing leadership organizations that inspire community connection, engagement, and attraction of qualified talent with shared visions. But more characteristically, Sandra has become heavily respected among her clients and peers for her transparent communication, compassionate ambiance, fierce business acumen, and ultimately for her unmatched commitment to exceeding expectations through each progressive stage.

To date, Sandra holds a BS Cum Laude in Accounting from Hunter College, a Juris Doctor Magna Cum Laude from Suffolk University Law School, and has attained several coinciding certifications, including (but not limited to) the Compliance & Ethics Professional certification from the Society of Corporate Compliance & Ethics. Sandra is also an avid public speaker and keynote presenter covering topics of leadership, DEI, employment, and retention, and she is an active affiliate and board member of several professional organizations. Her visionary attitude led to the formation of two local notable organizations: Georgia Haitian-American Chamber of Commerce and Haitian American Lawyers Association of Georgia.

Sandra is currently based in Atlanta, GA and is a mother of two daughters who inspire her to both be and do her best every single day.

Why I Wrote This Book

I wrote this book to empower Human Resource Coordinators for success!

The role of a Human Resources Coordinator (HRC) or Generalist is challenging.

As an HR professional, you are responsible for many tasks. You are usually the first point of contact for employees and managers who have questions about benefits, compensation, and other day-to-day issues.

Often, as an HRC, you will be responsible for conducting performance reviews, writing up disciplinary actions or terminations, and taking part in exit interviews with departing employees, all while handling various employment-related compliance matters on behalf of your organization. In addition to these duties, you will also manage employee files (including background checks), work on hiring processes, coordinate training programs, and serve as a key liaison between management and staff throughout the organization. All this can be challenging enough without having to deal with the added pressure of limited resources at hand!

HR coordinators are expected to wear many hats.

You are expected to wear many hats. You need to have a broad knowledge of all aspects of human resources, from hiring and firing employees to creating benefits packages, administering compensation plans and providing basic legal counsel. You are also responsible for managing people, projects, and budgets. Your communication skills need to be top-notch—you will often be the first point of contact for your company's employees or clients.

The job requires an ability to think critically about problems that arise within the organization and to find ways to solve them without disrupting business processes too much (or at all).

This guide is going to empower HRCs to do their jobs with more confidence and knowledge.

It will help you understand the role better, understand the importance of your role, the challenges you face, and most importantly empower you with practical approaches to properly manage the workforce from A to Z.

Now that you know a little more about what the role of the HRC is and why it's so important, let's get into the details.

Contents

Introduction

The Human Resources Coordinator (HRC) plays an extremely important role in ensuring an efficient and effective working environment through the consistent implementation of stellar and robust processes around the workforce management. This guide is designed to help you navigate the expectations of the role you have chosen to play in your workplace by providing you with resources.

This guide is divided into six main sections:

- Recruitment and Selection
- Onboarding and Orientation of New Employees
- Retention and Engagement
- Learning and Development
- Compensation and Benefits
- Compliance & Legal

Taking care of people is the business of HR professionals. This guide will help establish best practices to ensure that all staff members will be provided with adequate HR support and guidance to enable them to deliver the required services to their clients.

It is a best practice to prepare a contact list for new hires to make it easier for them to reach out to management when a problem arises. It is recommended that the contact list be generic and adaptable enough to allow new hires to fill out the information during their onsite orientation.

The contact list would generally allow for the name and contact information for supervisory or managerial officers of the company who can quickly provide support to new hires in case of an issue.

Recruitment

As the leader of talent acquisition at your organization, you probably already know that the best way to attract and retain top talent is by having a strong talent acquisition strategy. But how do you ensure that your organization's hiring process is as effective as possible? How can you ensure that your company's hires are aligned with its culture, mission and values? And how do you make sure they'll be a good fit for the job or role they're being hired into? These are all questions we've been asked many times before—and we're not surprised! After all, running an effective recruiting campaign is no easy feat.

That's why we created this guide on recruitment strategies: it contains everything from templates for creating jobs and posting them externally, to tips for making sure candidates get through every step of the process successfully (without any unnecessary red tape). We hope these resources help make hiring easier for both recruiters and HR professionals alike!

A great recruitment process starts with the identification of staffing needs for your workplace. Working with your workforce manager, scheduler, and attending a daily staffing needs meeting is required for such a process. In a staffing needs meeting, a checklist may be used to ensure a critical assessment of staffing needs happens on a daily basis.

The Human Resources Coordinator (HRC)

Human Resources Coordinator (HRC) is the first point of contact and the main resource for all HR activities. HRCs are responsible for coordinating all HR activities and ensuring that they are carried out in a timely manner. HRCs also ensure that all policy and procedure changes are communicated to employees, as well as making sure that any training needs are met. A human resources coordinator may also be responsible for managing employee relations issues such as complaints from employees or union representation; managing payroll functions including wages, taxes, deductions etc.; developing new systems/processes; recruiting employees; assisting with benefits administration.

Once staffing needs are identified, your company can use the following tools to effectively manage the recruitment of employees:

- Talent Acquisition Process Checklist – this should be used daily
- Sourcing Resources for Centers
- Internal Job Posting Template
- Job Fair Checklist
- Recruitment Bonuses (Referral, Sign-on, Conversion)

Your company is required to use the **Talent Acquisition Process Checklist** on a daily basis in order to timely connect with candidates who apply for open positions at the center. In preparation for the Daily Workforce Management meeting, the checklist should be reviewed and followed first thing in the morning every day.

Talent Acquisition Process Checklist

☀ Define roles and responsibilities

☀ Define goals

☀ Define metrics

☀ Determine timelines for each stage of the talent acquisition process, including:

- Recruitment process planning (this includes defining your recruiting strategy)

- Talent Acquisition Program implementation (recruiting tools and techniques)

- Candidate experience and tracking

- Onboarding new employees

- Determine resources needed to achieve your goals, including staffing budget or number of full-time equivalents (FTEs) needed to complete the project on time

Posting Openings

As openings and needs to replace those openings are identified, your company should immediately post a requisition in its Applicant Tracking Systems (ATS). To maximize exposure, it is recommended that requisitions for openings are refreshed a minimum of every two weeks. The reason to refresh those openings is that older openings send the wrong message to job seekers. If they see that a position has been opened for too long, they start wondering about the workplace culture and whether they would want to work there. Your recruiter supports the recruitment needs and is a great resource to your company. Accordingly, it is recommended that you create an open position report and that at least each week, that report is sent out to the management team and scheduler for timely updates. The report is a useful tool for verifying and confirming that you are working with an updated list of openings for your workplace.

Additionally, use of an **internal job posting template** to post openings on a job posting board is recommended. A HRC can work with management to create a job posting board in a conspicuous location that is accessible to all employees. Generally, a breakroom or lunchroom is an excellent location to have such a board. Employees spend time there to relax or to eat. That is ideally when they spend time perusing materials that are posted. Having a job board in a lunchroom is an excellent way to ensure that employees see the openings and are able to refer candidates. The HRC should work in tandem with the recruiter to ensure internal job postings are up to date and properly reflect current openings and bonuses offered in conjunction with the openings.

Sourcing Resources for Workplaces

A ll workplaces, but especially those in recruitment challenged areas, should foster relationships with **school counselors and representatives of career services** departments in their markets. HRCs should enlist the support of the management team and work with school directors to develop and maintain relationships with students and staff through on-site presentations, advertising job openings in local school publications, providing job flyers for school bulletin boards, and attending job fairs sponsored by the schools. Educational institutions with which to partner should include community colleges, high schools, local universities, and technical/trade schools.

You can find resources for your workplace in many places. There are online job boards, industry associations and conferences, social media sites like LinkedIn and Facebook, and industry publications. Many of these have job listings or a database of candidates.

- ☀ Online job boards: These are websites where employers post open positions and candidates upload their resumes or apply directly from the site. Examples include Monster.com, Indeed.com, and SimplyHired.com.

- ☀ Industry associations: Members of an association often seek out each other for advice about topics related to their field or specialization (also known as peer-to-peer networking). In addition to learning more about your field through educational events like conferences, you may be able to find potential employees through members who would be willing to recommend someone they know well; you could also advertise that your organization is hiring within the association's newsletter or even on its website itself!

- ☀ Social media networks: While not exclusively focused on employment opportunities like professional organizations can be—and thus not entirely reliable when it comes time actually filling out applications—these networks still serve as good starting points if nothing else seems promising after scouring other sources. TikTok, Reels on Instagram.

Additional sourcing resources could include anywhere the company would be allowed to post for openings, such as religious institutions, the department of labor, veteran sites, chambers of commerce, local charitable organizations that promote trade opportunities for the disenfranchised (for example shelters that support women who are encouraged to work), and possibly local YMCAs.

Internal Job Posting Template

- Include a job description summary.

- Include a list of required minimum skills and qualifications.

- Include a list of required minimum education and experience.

- Include a list of required technical skills.

- If shifts are relevant, it is important to include that as well.

For example, at a minimum, a job posting should include: looking for a 3p to 11p certified nursing assistant to work on a dementia unit. Interested candidates should have a valid certification, and at least 3 years' experience working with dementia patients in a controlled setting.

Job Fairs

At times, a company may have to avail itself of additional recruitment avenues. One such avenue is to either hold a job fair on-site or to participate in fairs that are happening in their communities. HRCs are encouraged to work with their management team to create a checklist they can use to routinely plan job fairs. A Job Fair Planning Process Checklist is a valuable, consistent tool to use to plan for a successful job fair. In addition, the Job Fair Process Checklist is a great resource to help your company think through all the tools needed to operationalize a successful job fair.

Job Fairs Checklist

- Is the job listed in a way that makes sense and is easy to read? (e.g., not too many details, no jargon, etc.)

- Is the job seeker able to find the requirements of the job (what are the hiring managers looking for)?

- Is there a list of qualifications that applicants need in order to be considered for an interview? (e.g., education level, experience level, etc.)

Recruitment Bonuses

Before publicizing a bonus program, HRCs should confirm with their management team whether the bonus program is still current to attract candidates. Companies often offer bonus programs as an incentive to secure new hires or to convert employees that work part time or per diem to regular Full-Time employees. All bonus programs must have prior approval from the relevant management line and/or budget holder. These programs are designed to improve and enhance a company's recruitment processes. Here are sample bonus programs that can be offered to candidates:

- ☀ **Sign-On Bonus** – The sign-on bonus is usually paid to a new hire. The sign-on bonus is designed to assist with hard-to-fill positions within a workplace. It is an attractive way to entice employees who are on the fence to leave another employer to come work for us. Sometimes, experienced workers are leaving benefits they have accrued over the years at another company. The Sign-On bonus provides them with additional pocket money that helps new hires with the transition to a new employer.

- **Conversion Bonus** –The conversion bonus is similar to sign-on bonuses in that it's mostly used when recruiting from within your company rather than external sources. This bonus is used when trying to convert employees from one role into another role within the same organization (e.g., sales rep into manager). The conversion bonus is also designed to help change the status of an employee; that is to convert fixed-term or part-time hires into full-time employees.

- **Referral Bonus** – This is an incentive paid to an internal employee who refers someone who is hired. The referred person or new hire may get a sign on bonus and the referring person, who is already an employee, will get the referral bonus. The referral bonus is designed to increase buy-in from current employees to participate in filling centers' openings. Payment of the referral bonus is generally predicated upon the new hire remaining an employee for a pre-determined period of time, for example six months or a year.

Keep in mind that with all the bonuses, the company may decide to pay the amount over time. That is the company may divide the bonus amount to be paid out in equal installments and not at all once. Therefore, it is very important for HRCs to check with their management team on not only the amount of the bonus but also on the cadence for payment.

In conclusion, the talent acquisition process is vital to ensuring that there is a candidate pipeline ready to supply the company with a qualified pool of applicants and candidates. Thus, HRCs need to constantly assess whether the process is working and whether tools and systems need to be revised and updated. HRCs should regularly strive to identify gaps, then perform root cause analyses and finally design an action plan to fill those gaps. In short, it is a best practice to

- Evaluate and reassess our talent acquisition process and systems continually
- Review the process and systems
- Evaluate the effectiveness of the process and systems
- Reassess the process and systems

Selection

The selection process is the time period during which candidates are contacted and interviewed leading to a potential job offer. It is paramount to identify early on all the stakeholders that will ensure a smooth candidate experience. HRCs' role is to ensure that the right hiring managers are included in the selection process. With the shortage in finding great talent, keep in mind that time is of the essence in the selection process. HRCs must coordinate the process to ensure the best candidate is hired within the shortest amount of time possible. Accordingly, it is a best practice to schedule panel interviews with all hiring managers rather than having candidates report several times to the workplace for interviews. The selection process entails the candidate selecting the company as an employer as well; it is not just about the company selecting the employee.

When hiring new employees, it's important to have a clear, equitable and efficient selection process.

This process should include:

1. Create a position description that put all persons involved in the process on notice regarding the requirements for the role

2. Ensure all hiring managers have access to interview guides that promote behavioral based interviews.

3. Define the offer, and the contingencies associated with an offer

Create a position description

Start with a position description that outlines what is expected from employees in this role. Having this tool for the hiring managers and the candidate will help ensure that all candidates receive equal treatment during interviews.

During the interview, using behavioral based questions provides better insight into the caliber of candidates. Because these types of questions are meant to gauge how candidates react to stress, and how they conduct themselves in a professional environment, they allow the interviewer to get a better and a greater understanding of the candidate. HRCs can work on designing STAR based tools to help managers gauge the answers they receive from candidates. The STAR method is a structured manner of responding to behavioral-based interview questions whereby the candidate is asked to discuss the specific situation, task, action, and result of the situation they are describing.

Ensure all candidates receive equal treatment.

In healthcare, it is important that all offers be contingent upon a successful background check, drug testing and references. The contingencies are different depending on the industry in which the company operates. HRCs need to research the general Ask for references from previous employers or professional referees if appropriate before making a final decision about who you want to employ.

Different employers have different standards as to whether they will provide a reference, and some may not be happy about giving references for staff members who have left their employment under circumstances that could reflect badly on them. In addition, many companies' policies state that employee references can only be given with written permission from the employee himself/herself—so it may not always be possible for you to get one anyway! Generally speaking, references should be limited to asking for dates of employment and role held at the prior place.

Prior employers may or may not answer questions regarding the whether they would rehire the candidate.

If you do receive references, make sure that they are recent ones (from within 12 months of applying) and relevant in scope (they should cover specific areas related to your job). Also, check with candidates what sort of things they would like included in any reference provided by an employer or colleague—this way there won't be any embarrassing surprises later down the line!

Offer the job and get written consent from your new employee before they start work.

Hiring is a crucial step in the life of a company. It's not just about bringing on new bodies to work on projects. It's about getting someone who can do their job well and contribute to the overall success of your organization. Making sure your hiring practices are as strong as possible is key to finding candidates with the skills and experience needed by your team, while also avoiding discriminatory hiring practices such as those based on gender identity or race/ethnicity (which could result in similar outcomes).

Hiring is a complicated process but having a clear and equitable process can help ensure that you hire the right person for the job.

It is recommended to have a regular staffing call designed to support recruiters and hiring managers in their recruitment efforts. On that call, attendees should be ready to discuss openings in their workplace and recruitment efforts they are engaged in. HR should work with the leadership or management team to determine the cadence of the calls.

Onboarding & Orientation

Onboarding

The process of bringing a new employee on board is often referred to as onboarding, and it's important for the success of both the company and the new hire. Onboarding is an opportunity to help employees understand their role in your business, get them acclimated to their new environment, and ensure they can contribute right away—while also reducing turnover rates. Onboarding occurs after an offer for employment has been extended, but subject to references and background checks being cleared.

Self-Identification Form

To comply with federal and state guidelines, it is required to collect and maintain certain information regarding applicants. The candidate should complete a Self-Disclosure Form along with an Application for Employment. Providing the requested information should be considered voluntary and will be used for statistical purposes only. This requirement is largely dependent on the industry and whether the company is considered a government contractor. In the government space, this survey is also used to collect EEO-1 data that is later used to create Affirmative Action Plans.

FCRA Authorization

For some selective positions, a company may require that a credit report be secured as part of the onboarding process. In those circumstances, during the onboarding process, the candidate must also complete an authorization and Fair Credit Reporting Act Disclosure form (FCRA). Retain FCRA forms in a confidential file that is separate from Employment Applications. The retention period is six years from the date of application.

What is a FCRA authorization?

A Federal Consumer Reporting Agency (FCRA) authorization is a document that allows you to access the information in a candidate's credit report. It also allows you to share this information with other companies, such as potential employers who are considering a candidate for a job opening. When candidates sign the FCRA authorizations, they give permission for their personal identifying information (PII) to be shared with third parties. This includes their name, address and Social Security number as well as any salary information on their credit report.

Why should I collect and store these authorizations?

The Fair Credit Reporting Act (FCRA) requires employers to obtain written consent before they can view or use an individual's consumer report – which includes credit reports – when making employment decisions like hiring or promotions. The goal of this requirement is twofold: firstly, it helps protect consumers from having their privacy violated by unauthorized accesses of their personal data; secondly, it helps maintain fairness between those who cannot afford services like background checks versus those who can pay for them directly instead of going through an employer who may use these types of services themselves.

Background Screening & Fingerprinting (Where Applicable)

Similarly, for some selected industries, especially those in healthcare, a background check and fingerprinting might be required of all candidates for employment. If that is the case, then the following process should be honored.

When a conditional offer has been extended, that is the time to initiate a criminal background screen. Most Applicant Tracking Systems allow this process to be completed in their systems. If a third-party vendor processes the background check, the ATS could probably be integrated with the vendor's system in order to more efficiently process these tests. Generally, upon completion of these tests, HR will receive an email notification indicating the process is complete. The email notification will state if the individual has passed or if the background check requires further review. If further review is required, the candidate is notified for follow up as necessitated by the vendor's process.

Some states require **fingerprinting** as part of the onboarding process. Fingerprinting is another option that many companies choose to use in conjunction with their background checks; some states and industries require fingerprinting before employment can begin, while others allow it as an option. Please speak to your management team about the criteria for your specific industry and state requirements.

Reference Checks

Reference checks are an essential part of the hiring process, helping you to verify a candidate's skills and experience. While it may seem daunting to contact references during the hiring process, it's actually quite straightforward. The best way to learn about someone's professional behavior is by asking them directly:

- Do you have any prior experience working with this person? How has it been?

- What were some of their strengths in the workplace? What are some areas they could improve upon?

- Would you hire them again? Why or why not?

As stated above, many employers are reluctant to provide detailed, explicit reference checks for prior employees. At times, references may just confirm dates of employment and a "yes" or "no" answer regarding the candidate's eligibility for rehire. HR could perform the reference checks or could outsource the task to a third-party vendor. Regardless of who completes it, the result of reference checks and other pre-employment tests should be stored in the employee's personnel file if hired.

Orientation

Team Member's First Day

A great first impression for new hires starts on day one, but it doesn't end there. Statistically, the majority of new hires leave within the first thirty (30) days of hire. Remember your first day of work or your first day of school? Were you nervous? Did you know anyone? Did you worry about failing or not being able to grasp the position for which you were hired? It is important to have processes in place to facilitate new hires' transition to the company. Paying attention to these details upfront, before they start, will help alleviate the angst of new hires and achieve retention goals.

All new hires should be expected to attend some sort of General Orientation on their first day of employment. General Orientation is the company's management team's opportunity to lay out the expectations for ALL new employees! This includes leadership hires, as well. An effective orientation starts with professionalism and preparedness. New hires who participate in a structured onboarding program are 69% more likely to stay with a company for 3 years. General Orientation is primarily a Human Resources (HR) function, which will be led by the HR team in the workplace; nonetheless, it requires the engagement of the entire leadership team for it to be impactful and effective.

Expectations for Orientation:

- Schedule general orientation on a consistent, regular day and time with the leadership team to encourage their participation and engagement.

- Roll out the red carpet for the new hires!

- Have their name badges ready for them.

- Have General Orientation folders ordered and available, including the Orientation Guides, Benefit Guides/Summary, as well as Employee Handbooks with pertinent policies

- Presenters should familiarize themselves with the material they will be presenting.

- Start orientation on time.

- Have the orientation room clean and organized (spruce it up with balloons, Pictures, Service Standard popup banner, etc.)

- Put together goodie bags for the new hires (company pens, giveaways, etc.)
- Pre-plan for how to make the orientation interactive such as having an icebreaker activity prepared and other activities to break up the day.

An Orientation Guide should be prepared for your company to use as a reference tool outlining a structured onboarding process. This will ensure that new hires are welcomed and integrated into the workplace. Additionally, having a guide allows for a thorough, well-planned orientation process, which tends to promote greater productivity, reduced turnover, leading ultimately to a more satisfied and engaged workforce. The guide also allows for consistency in the delivery of a standard orientation for all.

HR coordinators or generalists should follow a General Orientation Agenda. In case of a change in the schedule where a manager is unable to present, HR should be prepared to find alternative ways to cover the material on the agenda. Where alternate presenters are identified, remember to get them approved by the management team. It is recommended to have a list of pre-approved alternate presenters for those unexpected situations.

The general orientation is not meant to be all inclusive. The purpose of the general orientation is to introduce the new hire to the company and review general policies, with which the new hire needs to be familiar. Therefore, it is important that upon the completion of the general orientation, the new hire is presented with the opportunity to transition to their respective departmental orientation. The manager of that department should have an orientation checklist to follow.

Providing new hires with department specific orientation, in addition to a general orientation, positions the new hire for greater success in their roles with the company.

It is common knowledge that the highest turnover occurs during the first 90 days. Therefore, it is crucial to help support new hires during this important period with regular check-ins to quickly identify the challenges they encounter. The following is an example of a week-by-week transition plan to the floor for a new hire.

- ☀ Week 1:
    - Assign the new employee a mentor on their shift. Work with HR to help implement a mentor program in the workplace.
    - Facilitate daily follow-up with the new employee to determine further training needs or alternative training methods needed to assure success.
    - Create/Update a new hire welcome board whereby existing employees are encouraged to look for and to welcome the newly hired employees.
- ☀ Week 2:
    - Facilitate daily check-ins with the new hires and supervisors.
    - Adjust training as needed to address immediate challenges new hires may face.
    - Ensure new hire is acclimating to the work environment demands and has appropriate support with their workload.

During the second month, you should still check in with the new hires to identify and address any challenges they are experiencing. A great best practice is to meet with them at least every other week. Throughout the second and third months, the management team should continue to meet with new hires through regularly scheduled events such as:

- ☀ Meal with Management, or Soup with Supervisors, or Lounge with Leaders

Additional Tips for an effective onboarding and orientation process:

- ☀ New hires should feel welcomed as a part of the team before they arrive on their first day. Consistent follow-up post offer and during the onboarding process is essential.
- ☀ General Orientation should be well organized and participation of leadership employees is essential.

- Transitioning from a classroom orientation to their assigned area of work on the floor is a critical time to support new hires and thus regular check-ins should be maintained and followed without exception.

- Engagement by the leadership team during the first two weeks of hire is a critical step in the Red-Carpet philosophy. Each new employee should be assigned a "Leadership Buddy" that makes daily contact with them.

- Informal positive peer partners are also essential to a great new hire experience.

The implementation of the "Leadership Buddy" practice will alert you to areas of improvement and coaching opportunities for co-workers' behaviors toward each other. Addressing these issues immediately will result in clearer expectations for the team as a whole. Setting expectations of mission-oriented behavior for everyone is a best practice.

Retention & Engagement

Retention refers to the ability of an organization to retain its employees. "Employee Engagement" is defined as the strength of the mental and emotional connection employees feel toward their places of employment.

Engaged employees are those who are involved, enthusiastic, and committed to their work and their workplace. Having valuable and engaging retention strategies, both formal and informal, are important to the overall success of the team.

In addition to recognizing **birthdays and anniversaries** of employees, below are some retention and engagement activities. The ultimate goal of engaging in these activities is to facilitate a process within the workplace where employees feel they have a voice, they are acknowledged and appreciated. HR is encouraged to incorporate some of these activities in their workplace's retention plan to promote the retention of valuable employees.

- 💡 **Team Rounds** - Every day, for a few minutes, members of the leadership team should walk the halls and talk with employees, providing an opportunity to connect with and listen to employees.

- 💡 **Suggestions Box or Similar Outlets** - should be placed either in break rooms or outside of the HR office. All employees should be encouraged to use the suggestion box to either praise things that are going well or bring up things that need to be improved within the workplace. Employees should be presented with the option to either identify themselves or participate anonymously. The box or outlet – whether digital or manual - provides employees with the opportunity to communicate issues, concerns, thoughts, etc., and be heard. It is critical for the management team, supervisors, and HR also to develop a process to follow up with employees and act on issues that are raised. Otherwise, the suggestion box approach misses its intended purpose.

- 💡 **Social Media** – Social media pages like Facebook, LinkedIn, TikTok and others are great platforms to recognize employees' achievements.

After securing the employees' consent, HR could post photos of employees' activities in the workplace.

- 💡 **Appreciation Events** – celebratory events for employees could include cook-outs, Taco Tuesday, ice cream socials, food cook-off/bake-off competitions, Employee of the Month, and holiday celebrations. For workplaces with a highly diverse workforce, HR could facilitate potlucks for **International Days** where employees are encouraged to bring in dishes that represent their country of origin. It is important to create and work with an employee retention committee of some sort so that HR is not solely responsible for driving employee appreciation events in the workplace.

- 💡 **Individual Recognition of Remarkable Employees** - Thank you notes, especially handwritten on a card, from the leadership team recognizing an employee's dedication and hard work is a great retention tool. Employees need to know that supervisors and management see their contribution.

- **Surveys for Feedback** – HR professionals are encouraged to work with their leadership teams to develop surveys to get feedback from employees. Though there was mention of suggestion boxes earlier in this guide, the type of survey mentioned here is more structured and is done either at a specific point of time for a specific purpose or is conducted yearly to select feedback to strategize as part of an overall action plan for the workplace. The following is a list of surveys that can be conducted:

Anonymous survey to find out from employees' perspective areas that management is doing well as well as areas for improvement.

- First Impressions surveys for new hires

- Exit interviews

- Stay interviews

- Ensure an open-door policy so all employees are comfortable coming in and talking about their concerns.

- Implement team building events in the workplace with all employees. Friendly competition among various units or departments to address impacting operational metrics such as attendance or quality is encouraged. Leadership should then recognize the unit or department that had the most positive impact on the targeted metrics.

HR professionals should also work with the leadership team in their workplace to create a Spirit or Retention Committee. As mentioned above, in addition to ensuring that employees and not HR lead this committee, the purpose of the committee is to periodically review recruitment and retention needs for the workplace and incorporate activities that could benefit them. This guide, in the sections discussed above, is replete of recruitment and retention activities that HR professionals could introduce to the committee for discussion around those activities that are most impactful to the workplace.

Ideas discussed in the committee meeting should be captured and reviewed with the management team. From there, the company leadership team could work with the management team to implement an action plan to address areas of concern. To be achievable, an action plan should address one or two goals with 3-5 action steps for each goal. The plan should not be an exhaustive list of all the things that could be corrected. Rather, it should be a strategic dynamic document with SMART action items that can be implemented and measured for impact on recruitment, turnover, retention, and employee engagement.

Learning and Development

Management and leadership are two of the most important drivers of employee recruitment, retention, and engagement. Very often, front-line managers are promoted into their positions with little if any preparation on how to lead a team thereby constituting a key factor in turnover among employees. Therefore, it is critical to invest in managers and supervisors' continued growth as leaders.

Companies should endeavor to support professional growth by assessing their employees' training needs. By identifying gaps in skills and knowledge, the company can create an actionable plan for each employee to fill those gaps. This allows for a more streamlined approach to learning, which creates a more effective learning environment for everyone involved.

Assess employees' training needs

To assess employees' training needs, a company should first identify the areas they wish employees to be proficient in throughout their employment with the company (e.g., become proficient with social media marketing tools). As part of the assessment, companies should test how confident employees are in their ability to complete related tasks on their own, without significant coaching or guidance from management or leadership teams. This exercise will provide leaders with insight into how well-equipped employees are in their current roles compared to their readiness to ascend to a higher role. Finally, after analyzing all test results, leaders will be able to compare confidence level vs. actual skill level, and create actionable plans aimed at developing employees.

Offer a curated, relevant selection of courses

Companies should offer a curated platform of training materials to their employees. The process of curation ensures that the company's Learning & Development selection includes only the most relevant courses for the company and its employees. Companies should be intentional in creating a learning menu that caters to their employees' needs to live and manifest the company's mission and core values and to effectively perform their jobs as relevant to their roles.

Provide courses at multiple levels of expertise

It's important to provide courses at multiple levels of expertise. You should have beginner, intermediate, and advanced courses that correspond to different levels of proficiency. If you only teach beginners and novices, you will leave out a large portion of your workforce that could benefit from becoming more skilled.

If your company has multiple roles (e.g., salespeople vs. product developers), then it makes sense to create learning paths based on these roles and the competencies within each role. By organizing your learning programs this way, it'll be clear what resources people need in order to reach their current goals or progress within their careers.

Include both online and in-person learning opportunities

The best way to learn is by doing. A group setting gives you the opportunity to participate, ask questions, and get feedback from coworkers who have already been through the training or are currently working on it. You can build relationships with people who may want to refer you for projects in the future or even recommend your company as a place where they would like to work.

In-person learning also allows employees in different roles and departments at your organization to share their knowledge with each other - this helps create more collaborative teams that are stronger than any one person alone could be.

Offer online resources to reinforce key learning points

- Online resources can be used to reinforce key learning points.

- Online resources can be used to provide additional information, practice, and support.

- Online resources can also be a great motivational tool!

- Ensure the learning platform is accessible

- Make sure the learning platform is accessible from any device, including desktops, laptops, tablets and smartphones. Employees should be able to log in from a room full of their colleagues during a meeting or on their own time at home after work.

- Ensure the platform is easy to use and navigate so that learners won't get lost when looking for content or taking courses.

- Training should also include an easy-to-use search feature that allows employees to easily find what they're looking for within your training catalog (i.e., not just searching for "management skills" but also "managing teams").

Encourage employees to share what they learn

You can help employees to learn and retain the most essential information by encouraging them to share what they're learning with their colleagues.

- Sharing what you learn helps you retain information. Even when we think we understand something well, many of us find that sharing it makes us remember it better—and connecting ideas is one way to do that.

- Sharing what you learn is an excellent way to make connections between ideas and people. The more connections a person makes between concepts or ideas, the easier it is for them to put things into context; this context helps with recall later on when they need those concepts again (which is almost always).

Learning and development programs are important drivers of team member satisfaction, engagement, and retention.

As they become increasingly more important drivers of employee satisfaction and engagement, learning and development programs are a primary way that companies can keep their people happy. We've found that employees are far more likely to stay at a company if they feel like they are growing both personally and professionally.

In fact, according to some studies, employees who feel that their employer cares about them are:

- Four (4) times as likely to be engaged in their work
- Eight (8) times as likely to recommend the company as an employer

An online learning system should be available to all employees. This system provides education sessions essential to employees' specific positions. In addition to increasing the employees' professional and functional skills, the courses are designed to meet regulatory requirements for certifications, licensures, or registrations. Consistent use of our learning and development platform allows the Company to identify managers and leaders, improve development plans for line staff and managers, as well as mitigate managerial risks involved in leading the business.

If all of these best practices sound like a lot of work to you, don't worry. Your organization doesn't have to implement every single one at once. In fact, it may be better if you take things slowly and start with just a few that fit your particular needs as an employer. And remember: the most important part of learning and development is having a strong commitment from senior leadership that this is going to be important for them in the long term—and then taking action on those words.

Compensation & Benefits

A company's compensation and benefits strategy is an important element of its total rewards program. Effective compensation strategies help to attract and retain top talent, while effective benefits strategies help employees feel valued. This guide will walk you through what makes up a solid compensation and benefits package and provide step-by-step instructions on how to develop your own strategy.

It is essential for an organization to have a fair and transparent system for all staff. Your company should always ensure that they are using the **most updated wage scales** for the recruitment of direct care employees.

Payroll

HRCs are generally responsible for processing payroll timely and correctly. It is important that employees are paid on time and for all hours worked. There should be payroll guides with clear processes that are documented with expectations regarding how employees hours are documented and verified, consistent deadlines for employees to review their hours and ensure they are correct so that payroll is completed timely.

Create a compensation and benefits strategy that is aligned with your company's goals.

Although compensation is an important part of the total rewards package, benefits are equally important.

Benefits can be used to attract and retain employees, but they also have a more subtle role: helping employees save for retirement or cover medical expenses. In addition, some benefits can help you meet your company's goals. For example:

- ۞ A health insurance plan can help reduce employee turnover by giving employees peace of mind that they will be able to continue receiving care if they get sick or injured.

- ۞ Retirement plans enable employees to save money on their own terms while simultaneously providing employers with tax savings through matching contributions or profit-sharing opportunities (depending on what plan you choose).

When devising your benefits strategy, make sure to provide for all elements of total rewards.

Total rewards is defined as the total of all non-monetary benefits provided by an employer, including those provided through a company's medical plan and 401(k) plan. Benefits can include health insurance, life insurance, disability insurance, and retirement savings options.

When devising your company's benefits strategy, it's important to consider all elements of total rewards—including base pay, incentives, and other compensation items such as paid time off (PTO) or vacation days—as well as non-cash benefits like health insurance or a 401(k). A strong benefits offering can help attract top talent on its own merits while also serving to retain current employees who may have been considering leaving for other companies offering better packages elsewhere.

Be sure to provide basic insurance plans, such as medical and dental insurance.

As a small business owner, you may be tempted to overlook the need for basic insurance plans. However, if you don't provide them, your employees will likely find their own coverage elsewhere. In addition to medical and dental insurance, consider providing accidental coverage; critical illness coverage; life insurance plans; short-term disability and long-term disability benefits.

Offering optional voluntary benefits can help employees feel like they have greater control over their benefits.

Voluntary benefits, also called flexible benefits or employee-funded benefits, are those that employees can choose to enroll in if they want. This gives employees more control over the design of their benefit package and often makes them feel like the company cares about their wellbeing.

Some examples of voluntary benefits include:

- Flexible spending accounts (FSAs) - FSAs allow employees to set aside money from their paychecks on a pre-tax basis for medical expenses not covered by insurance, such as dental care and prescription medication. Enrolling in an FSA allows employees to take advantage of tax savings while still having access to coverage when needed.

- Health Savings Accounts (HSAs) - HSAs are similar to FSAs but with higher contribution limits and greater flexibility around how funds are used (for example, you can use your HSA funds toward both medical expenses and out-of-pocket healthcare costs).

Enrollment should be easy and benefit options should be clearly spelled out.

Enrolling your employees in the right benefits should be easy, and benefit options should be clearly spelled out. Employees should understand exactly how each benefit works, what they're getting out of it, and why it's important to them. They'll also want to know if there are any restrictions on their participation or limitations on what they can receive from the plan.

In addition to making enrollment easy for employees by providing simple forms or online portals where people can enroll themselves or get help from a representative, employers need to make sure that benefits are communicated clearly—both when explaining them during enrollment as well as throughout the year after an employee has signed up for coverage.

Have multiple communication channels available to employees.

It's important to have multiple communication channels available to employees. This will help you avoid confusion and frustration in the workplace. Some examples include:

- Email

- Websites and intranet sites

- Social media (Twitter, Facebook, Instagram)

It is also important that employees have access to information about their benefits and how they can enroll in them. Employees should be able to communicate with the HR team directly via phone or live chat if they need more information or clarification on any aspect of their benefit plan.

Communicate the value of the benefits being offered.

Keep in mind that, although your employees are all different, they all have one thing in common—they want to know the value of the benefits being offered. The more you can explain why your benefits are important and how they work, the better. It's also helpful for employees to know that there are other sources for information about your employee benefits packages, such as:

- ☀ Your internal website or intranet site
- ☀ Benefits boards in lunch or break rooms

A well-developed compensation and benefits strategy can help you attract and retain top talent for your company.

Compensation and benefits are important for attracting and retaining top talent. But they can also be used as a recruiting tool, by showing prospective employees that your company is invested in their well-being. When it comes to compensation, you should make sure that your total rewards package is competitive with other companies in your industry. This will help you attract the best applicants who value their salary and benefits package enough to accept an offer from you over another company. Beyond this, it's important to consider the different aspects of your total rewards package when designing an employee retention strategy:

- ☀ Salary
- ☀ Bonus plans or profit-sharing plans
- ☀ Stock options or stock purchase plans (for example: "Employees who have been here one year will receive 10% off their next paycheck") (for example: "Employees who have been here two years will receive 15% off their next

paycheck") (for example: "Employees who have been here three years will receive 20% off their next paycheck")

The best compensation and benefits programs are those that reflect the needs of your company's employees. A good strategy will ensure that employees feel valued, keep them engaged at work, and help you attract top talent.

Benefits constitute the other part of employees' total compensation package.

Benefits are a great way to attract candidates and retain employees. They can also be a key part of companies' employee recruitment strategies, as more employers seek out candidates who are attracted to the benefits that a particular company offers. In this post, we'll explore different types of benefits companies offer, including medical insurance and dental care plans; accident coverage; critical illness coverage; life insurance plans; short and long term disability plans; paid holidays, vacation time, sick time and bereavement days off with pay; tuition reimbursement programs; commuter benefits like mass transit subsidies or vanpools; employee assistance programs (EAPs); retirement savings programs like 401(k)s or 403(b)s; child-related expenses such as daycare after-school programs offered by some employers.

Here are some sample benefits that are being offered to employees:

Medical Insurance

Medical insurance is a type of insurance that can help you pay for medical expenses if you get sick or injured.

Some companies offer medical insurance as a way to attract candidates, but the cost of it may be too expensive for some people. In this case, you may want to consider using a health savings account (HSA).

- ☀ Dental insurance

- Accident coverage: This benefit is designed to help protect covered individuals and their families against the unexpected expenses associated with certain accidents.

- Critical illness coverage: This type of insurance designed to help you cope with the financial consequences of certain life-changing health events. Critical illnesses are those that cause severe disability or death, and can include:

  - cancer

  - stroke

  - heart attack

  - organ failure (kidney, liver)

  - paralysis or brain damage caused by accident or surgery, etc.

Critical illness coverage tends to be one of the more expensive options on the market because it covers such a wide range of potential illnesses, but it's important to note that not everyone will qualify for this type of plan. Employees may need to meet age requirements as well as other limits placed on who can buy into these.

- **Life insurance plans**
- **Short and long-term disability**
- **Paid holidays**
- **Vacation time**
- **Sick time**
- **Bereavement**
- **Tuition Reimbursement benefits**

Companies should strive to remain competitive with their total rewards package for employees. It is not always possible to increase base salaries or wages. However, creative out of the box solutions can be used. There are several companies that now offer total rewards to companies at no cost to employers. Employers simply need to choose which benefits they want and allow the third-party vendor access to the employees.

HR Coordinators need to attend HR conferences or receive HR materials from organizations like SHRM and others in order to remain updated about offerings in the marketplace. Additionally, as the voice of the internal customer, HR Coordinators should ensure that surveys are being conducted to ask the employees what benefits they want their employers to offer them. Don't just assume that you know what employees want. Ask them and they will tell you!! Your compensation and benefits strategy will be more impactful because it would have reflected what your employees say they want.

Compliance & Legal

H R plays an important role in ensuring the workplace is compliant with laws and regulations pertaining to HR operations. In fact, an effectively run HR department can be a strategic cost saving partner to operations. During the life cycle of an employee, the employer needs to be conscious of areas that could lead to potential legal issues. Those include:

- Recruiting and Hiring – types of questions that can be asked, for example, during an interview. Accommodation must be provided to candidates who are disabled.

- Collecting and Using Employee Information – ensuring that confidential documents are kept in locked cabinets and that medical files are maintained separately. Additionally, ensure that, when key personal data of employees are being shared, the data is encrypted and is shared to only those who need the data for a business purpose.

- Availability and Preservation of Employment Records – there are specific retention periods for employment records. The HRC should work with their legal department or research on their own the proper retention periods for various employment records. State and federal laws may apply to access to employment records.

- Investigation of Wrongful Conduct – When allegations of wrongful conduct are brought to HR, it is paramount that responsible parties conduct full and thorough investigations into the allegations to ensure that company policies are followed.

- Discipline and Termination – great care should be placed in making sure that the progressive discipline process is followed. Deviation from policy can often lead to claims of unfair treatment and/or discrimination.

- Harassment and Discrimination – those claims must be worked on in collaboration with the leaders of your company and the legal department. If there is no legal department, it is important to discuss with management when to bring in an attorney to assist with the investigation into these claims.

- Personnel files – HRCs should ensure that each employee has a complete personnel file in the center. It is recommended to create a personnel file checklist that will outline the documents that are required to be in each employee file.

- DOL required postings in the centers should be conspicuously displayed in break rooms or near time clocks. Be sure to check the state department of labor website to determine the required posters for the state in which you operate.

Claims into non-payment of work hours or OT should always be investigated and promptly remedied. It is a great area of potential noncompliance that could result in double liability for the company.

Other potentially litigious areas include:

- UCSIS (U.S. Citizenship and Immigration Services)
    - I-9 Form (Employment Eligibility Verification Form)
    - eVerify (required by federal contractors and where state mandates; for example, the State of Alabama mandates eVerify by all employers)
- EEOC (Equal Employment Opportunity Commission)
    - Title VII of the Civil Rights Act of 1964 – harassment, national origin, pregnancy, race, religion, retaliation, sex/gender
    - ADEA (Age Discrimination in Employment Act) - age
    - ADA (Americans with Disabilities Act) - disability
- DOL (U.S. Department of Labor)
    - FLSA (Fair Labor Standards Act) – overtime, working off the clock, wage and hour
    - FMLA (Family and Medical Leave Act) – includes leaves of absence, paid or unpaid
    - USERRA (Uniformed Services Employment and Reemployment Rights Act)
- OSHA (Occupational Safety and Health Act of 1970)
    - Workers Compensation – employees that are injured on the job. Contact Workers Compensation for help with how to process claims that arise. See the Contact list at the beginning of this guide.

- NLRA (National Labor Relations Act)
  - NLRA – deals primarily with union-related issues. Reach out immediately to your upper management team with any concerns arising from a collective bargaining agreement or employees' grievances.

    For non-union related concerns, keep in mind that the NLRA forbids employers from preventing employees from discussing terms and conditions of employment.

HR representatives are recommended to conduct an audit into these potential risk areas and consult with legal if anything jumps at them that requires follow-up. Reach out to the Jean Consulting Group for these types of audit reviews to ensure the company is in legal compliance and not subject to potential expensive fines or litigation.

Appendix

Case Studies

Case Study #1

Maintaining and disseminating a comprehensive policy against discrimination and harassment can be a lifesaver for employers when faced with such claims.

In Banks v City of Atlanta, the Eleventh Circuit affirmed summary judgment for the city and dismissed claims of sexual harassment filed by four employees.

The court found that, viewing the facts in the light most favorable to the employees, summary judgement was warranted. The court found "specifically, the record shows that the City introduced uncontroverted evidence that it maintained a database through which all employees could access its policies. In addition, the City distributed its policies to employees at new-hire orientation, and it also provided an "alert" to all employees regarding updates to its policies which included a directive instructing employees to read the updated policies. Despite the Plaintiffs' argument that the general manager lacked awareness of the policy and had not received sexual harassment training, because the City adopted an anti-harassment policy that was comprehensive, well-known to most employees, and provided alternate avenues of redress, it is insulated from liability for the Plaintiffs' Title VII claims premised on constructive knowledge."

Case Study #2

Today let's talk about leave policies.

You hired Beth and she started working for you three months ago. She is quite the team member. Everyone loves Beth. Three months and a day within her employment, she shares that she is with child and her doctor wants her on intermittent leave.

Your immediate reaction is that she is so new and her position is so critical to the success of the team. What to do?

No matter the size of a company, business owners should have a well drafted employee handbook that contains, among other things, a leave policy.

When an employee needs to take a leave of absence, having a leave policy provides clarity and sets expectations, while also minimizing risks for the employer.

There are several types of leaves that an employee could request. However, keep in mind that not all types of leaves apply to all employers. Additionally, some common leaves such as maternity or disability leave, are governed by legislation.

Here are a few things to think about including in a leave policy:

    **Who is eligible for leave?

    **What are the minimum and maximum lengths of time for a leave of absence?

    **Is the leave paid or unpaid?

    **How do employees accrue leave?

    **How often can a single employee take a leave of absence?

To best know how to deal with Beth's or any other similar employee situations, don't stay exposed and risk making a decision that could lead to a lawsuit. Reach out to your transformational Business HR & Legal partner, The Jean Consulting Group, and let us help you keep your hard-earned money.

Case Study #3

$935,000!!

Plus attorney fees

Plus distraction from the daily operation of your business

Plus costs to become compliant

As well as intangible financial damage to your reputation...

That's how much it costs a company that failed to understand the need to assess and evaluate its workforce and take measures necessary to comply with employment laws.

Recently, Chris the Crazy Trader, Inc., doing business as Christopher's Dodge Ram in Golden, Colorado, has agreed to conciliate a discrimination charge involving failure to hire females with the U.S. Equal Employment Opportunity Commission (EEOC), the federal agency announced today.

The EEOC determined that Christopher Dodge Ram did not hire females for sales positions and did not keep records in violation of Title VII of the Civil Rights Act of 1964, as amended.

Christopher Dodge Ram has agreed to pay $935,000 to females affected by the discriminatory action.

In addition to the monetary compensation, Christopher Dodge Ram will work to increase female representation; hire an independent monitor; provide EEO training to all employees, including management; immediately change its hiring/record-keeping practices; and post a notice, in public view of the dealership lobby, that informs customers of their commitment to creating a workplace free from discrimination.

Here at the Jean Consulting Group LLC, we work with our clients to ensure compliance with regulatory requirements so they can keep their hard-earned money. Book a consultation with us and find out how we can add value to your business operations.

Case Study #4

Have you conducted a recent analysis of your employees' compensation?

It is a well-known fact that men are better at negotiating their compensation packages and women generally sell themselves short.

Nonetheless, employers be forewarned: discriminatory pay practices can cost your business beaucoup money. "Employers are required to pay male and female workers equally for equal work," said Gregory Gochanour, EEOC's regional attorney in Chicago. "That is the law, and the EEOC will hold employers accountable if they don't live up to that responsibility."

Recently Lacey's Place LLC Series Midlothian, doing business as Lacey's Place, which owns and operates more than 30 video gaming parlors in Illinois, was found to have violated civil rights law by paying female district managers lower wages than male district managers on the basis of sex, the U.S. Equal Employment Opportunity Commission (EEOC) charged in a lawsuit it filed today.

According to EEOC's lawsuit, female district managers were paid less than their male coworkers since at least March 2018. Several female district managers had similar or more experience and education than their male colleagues but made between $6,000 and $16,500 less in annual salary.

EEOC Chicago District Director Julianne Bowman stated, "The fact that we continue to see these sex-based wage disparities nearly 60 years after the Equal Pay Act and Title VII were enacted demonstrates that more work is required to achieve the promise of equal pay for equal work."

The EEOC is seeking back pay, liquidated damages, the elimination of pay disparities, and other injunctive relief to correct and prevent future pay discrimination.

Case Study #5

Ever heard of GINA?

GINA is not your lost cousin's newborn baby or newest girlfriend.

GINA stands for the Genetic Information Non-discrimination Act.

GINA essentially prohibits employers from requesting, requiring or purchasing genetic information about applicants or employees and their family members, except in very narrow circumstances. GINA defines "genetic information" to include the manifestation of a disease or disorder in an employee's family members.

Recently a medical practice company had to settle with the EEOC which found the employer in violation of GINA when it began collecting employees' family members' COVID-19 testing results. The company wanted to do the right thing but went about it the wrong way.

There is a sleuth of regulations from OSHA, EEOC, CMS, and others that govern the workforce. Don't take the chance of being in violation of any of them. Have a competent attorney review your rules and policies to mitigate your risks of being out of compliance and having to shell out tens of thousands of your hard-earned money.

Conclusion

Consistent and regular use of this guide will help position HRCs to be successful in their role in promoting their centers as the employer of choice in their markets.

As your role evolves, visit our website https://sandraljean.com/ for additional updates to this handbook and resources.

As you engage in hiring initiatives and demonstrate success in your role, keep us posted on how we can help or what could be improved upon to support you better! This is a great way to ensure we are doing our job well and staying current with industry trends.

You can always reach out to The Jean Consulting Group, LLC for guidance, training and leadership development. We're eager to partner with you as you grow within your position and at your organization.

Printed in Great Britain
by Amazon

24724948R00039